Roz ka Khana

TARLA DALAL
India's #1 Cookery Author

SANJAY & CO.
MUMBAI

Eighth Printing : 2007

ISBN 10 : 81-86469-35-4
ISBN 13 : 978-8-186469-35-4

Price: Rs. 89/-

Published & Distributed by : **Sanjay & Company**

353/A-1, Shah & Nahar Industrial Estate, Dhanraj Mill Compound, Lower Parel (W), Mumbai - 400 013. INDIA.
Tel. : (91-22) 2496 8068 • Fax : (91-22) 2496 5876 • E-mail : sanjay@tarladalal.com

---

UK and USA customers can call us on :
UK : 02080029533 ● USA : 213-634-1406
For books, Membership on **tarladalal.com**, Subscription for **Cooking & More** and Recipe queries
Timing : 9.30 a.m. to 7.00 p.m. (IST), from Monday to Saturday
Local call charges applicable

Recipe Research & Production Design	**Copy Editor**	**Photography**	**Design**
Pinky Chandan Dixit	Nisha Katira	Jignesh Jhaveri	Satyamangal Rege
Arati Fedane	**Food Styling**	**Typesetting**	**Printed by**
Jyoti Jain	Shubhangi Dhaimade	Adityas Enterprises	Minal Sales Agencies, Mumbai

DISCLAIMER
While every precaution has been taken in the preparation of this book, the publishers and the author assume no responsibility for errors or omissions. Neither is any liability assumed for damages resulting from the use of information contained herein. And of course, no book is a substitute for a qualified medical advice. So it is wiser to modify your dietary patterns under the supervision of a doctor or a nutritionist.

BULK PURCHASES
Tarla Dalal Cookbooks are ideal gifts. If you are interested in buying more than 500 assorted copies of Tarla Dalal Cookbooks at special prices, please contact us at 91-22-2496 8068 or email : sanjay@tarladalal.com

~ INTRODUCTION ~

With the advent of an enthusiastic trend among people to explore and appreciate delicacies from different parts of India, gone are the days when people stuck to their traditional food. Today's home-maker takes pride in presenting a variety of dishes to her family. A serious practical problem in doing so is the fear that a lot of time would be required for making such dishes. This book is intended to help the average hostess to overcome any such apprehensions.

The recipes introduced in this book have been prepared using readily available ingredients. I have taken care to see that all the recipes are very simple to prepare yet exotic in taste so as to enable you and your family to enjoy wonderful, wholesome and satisfying meals every day.

There is a wide array of dishes to choose from which you can fit into your daily menus be it the Paneer Potli ki Curry which has paneer potlis simmered in coconut gravy or the Badshahi Khichdi which is a meal by itself. Farsans like Dhokla Simla Mirch and Vegetable Rice Cakes are dishes you can rustle up in minutes. The methods of cooking suggested are simple, straight forward, not very time-consuming and above all, economical. Each recipe is formulated keeping in mind today's pace of living.

HAPPY COOKING !

Tarla Dalal

~ CONTENTS ~

DALS

[7 delightful ways to "pep" up your daily dals. One for each day of the week.]

RICE

[Versatile rice preparations that are sure to please your family.]

SUBZIS

[Delectable, easy to make vegetable preparations using common ingredients.]

FARSANS

[*These can add a little more variety to the regular dal-chawal meals or can even be served as snacks.*]

ROTIS

[*The addition of vegetable and pulses to your rotis provides variety as well as increases their nutritive value.*]

MITHAI

[*5 great recipes for mithais that are ready in a jiffy and cost effective too.*]

ACCOMPANIMENTS

[*Team these up with the parathas or the spicy rice preparations. You would not need to make a dal or a subzi.*]

Dals

~ Tamatar ki Kadhi ~

A simple tomato based curry.

Preparation time : 10 minutes.   Cooking time : 30 minutes.   Serves 4.

4 large tomatoes
½ tsp mustard seeds (rai)
½ tsp cumin seeds (jeera)
1 green chilli, chopped
5 to 6 curry leaves
2 cloves (laung)
2 tbsp Bengal gram flour (besan)
¼ tsp turmeric powder (haldi)
2 tsp chilli powder
a pinch asafoetida (hing)
2 tbsp grated jaggery (gur)
2 tbsp oil
salt to taste

For the garnish
1 tbsp chopped coriander

1. Roughly chop the tomatoes and cook them with ½ cup of water for about 10 to 15 minutes.
2. Cool and liquidize in a food processor to get a smooth purée. Keep aside.
3. Heat the oil in a saucepan and add the mustard seeds and cumin seeds. When they crackle, add the green chilli, curry leaves, cloves and gram flour and cook for 2 to 3 minutes.
4. Add the turmeric powder, chilli powder, asafoetida and puréed tomatoes with 2 cups of water and cook on a medium flame, stirring continuously.
5. When the kadhi comes to a boil, add the jaggery and salt and simmer for another 5 minutes.
6. Remove from the fire.
   Garnish with the chopped coriander and serve hot with rice.

~ Dal Kadhi ~

Chana dal and curds together make this delicious kadhi.

Preparation time : 10 minutes.   Cooking time : 30 minutes.   Serves 4.

1 cup split Bengal gram (chana dal)
1 tsp cumin seeds (jeera)
¼ tsp asafoetida (hing)
1 tsp ginger-green chilli paste
¼ cup finely chopped capsicum
1 tsp chilli powder
¾ cup curds, whisked
1 tsp sugar
¼ cup chopped coriander
1 tbsp oil
salt to taste

1. Wash and soak the Bengal gram in warm water for about 30 minutes. Drain and keep aside.

11

2. Add 2 cups of water and pressure cook the dal till it is tender.
3. Heat the oil in a saucepan and add the cumin seeds. When they crackle, add the asafoetida and ginger-green chilli paste and sauté for a few minutes.
4. Add the capsicum and chilli powder and stir-fry for some more time.
5. Add the dal and salt and simmer for about 5 minutes.
6. Remove from the fire. Add the curds, sugar and coriander and mix well. Serve hot.

~ **Subzi Dal** ~

A combination of pulses simmered with vegetables.

Preparation time : 15 minutes.   Cooking time : 30 minutes.   Serves 4.

⅓ cup yellow moong dal (split yellow gram)
⅓ cup toovar (arhar) dal
⅓ cup masoor dal (split red lentils)
½ tsp mustard seeds (rai)
½ tsp cumin seeds (jeera)
6 to 8 curry leaves
¼ tsp asafoetida (hing)
1 green chilli, chopped
1 onion, chopped
2 tsp ginger- green chilli paste
½ tsp garlic paste
1 large tomato, finely chopped
½ tsp chilli powder
½ tsp turmeric powder (haldi)

1 cup finely chopped mixed vegetables (capsicum, carrots, peas)
1 tbsp oil
salt to taste

For the garnish
2 tbsp chopped coriander

1. Wash and pressure cook the dals together with 2 cups of water till the dals are tender. Keep aside.
2. Heat the oil in a pan and add the mustard seeds and cumin seeds. When they crackle, add the curry leaves and asafoetida.
3. Add the green chilli and onions and sauté for 3 to 4 minutes.
4. Add the ginger-green chilli paste, garlic paste and tomato and sauté for 3 to 4 more minutes.
5. Add the chilli powder, turmeric powder and mixed vegetables and mix well.
6. Add the dals and salt and simmer for 5 to 10 minutes.
   Garnish with the chopped coriander and serve hot.

Handy Tip : You can use any left-over vegetable or curry instead of the mixed vegetables. This way you will have a different flavour each time.

～ **Palak Kofta Kadhi** ～

S*pinach dumplings simmered in a yoghurt curry.*

Preparation time : 15 minutes.   Cooking time : 20 minutes.   Serves 4.

For the palak koftas
1 cup spinach (palak) leaves, blanched, drained and chopped
¼ cup Bengal gram flour (besan)
½ tsp chilli powder
½ tsp cumin seeds (jeera)
a pinch soda bi-carb
salt to taste
oil for deep frying

For the kadhi
1 cup curds
2 tbsp Bengal gram flour (besan)
1 tsp cumin seeds (jeera)
a pinch asafoetida (hing)

5 curry leaves
1 onion, sliced
2 cloves garlic, finely chopped
¼ tsp turmeric powder (haldi)
1 tbsp oil
salt to taste

For the palak koftas
1. Mix the spinach leaves, gram flour, chilli powder, cumin seeds, soda bi-carb and salt in a bowl to get a soft dough.
2. Mix well, divide into 16 equal portions and shape into even-sized rounds.
3. Heat oil in a kadai and deep fry the koftas.
4. Remove and drain on absorbent paper. Keep aside.

For the kadhi
1. Mix the curds and gram flour in a bowl. Keep aside.
2. Heat the oil in a saucepan and add the cumin seeds. When they crackle, add the asafoetida, curry leaves, onion and garlic and sauté for 4 to 5 minutes.
3. Add the curds and gram flour mixture, turmeric powder, salt and 1 cup of water and bring to a boil.

How to proceed

Add the palak koftas to the hot kadhi and simmer for 4 to 5 minutes.
Serve hot with rice.

~ **Paneer Potli ki Curry** ~

Paneer palak potlis simmered in a coconut sauce.

Preparation time : 20 minutes.   Cooking time : 30 minutes.   Serves 4.

For the palak potlis
4 tbsp whole wheat flour (gehun ka atta)
4 tbsp spinach (palak), cooked and puréed
2 tsp oil
salt to taste

To be mixed into a stuffing mixture
2 tbsp grated paneer (cottage cheese)
2 tbsp chopped coriander
1 green chilli, finely chopped
salt to taste

CAULIFLOWER AND POTATO GHASI : Recipe on page 45 →

For the coconut sauce
2 cups (400 ml.) coconut milk
4 tsp cornflour
1 stick cinnamon (dalchini)
1 tsp cumin seeds (jeera)
4 to 6 curry leaves
2 tsp ginger-green chilli paste
1 tsp sugar
2 tsp lemon juice
2 tbsp oil
salt to taste

For the palak potlis
1. Mix all the ingredients in a bowl and make a firm dough, using water only if necessary.
2. Divide the dough into 24 portions.
3. Roll out each portion as thinly as you can into a circle of approx. 25 mm. (1") diameter.
4. Place ½ tsp of the stuffing mixture in the centre of each circle.
5. Brush the sides of the circles with a little cold water and seal the edges to make potlis (i.e. money bags). Keep aside.

For the coconut sauce

1. Dissolve the cornflour in 2 tbsp of water and add it to the coconut milk. Mix well and keep aside.
2. Heat the oil in a saucepan, add the cinnamon, cumin seeds and curry leaves and when the cumin seeds crackle, add the ginger-green chilli paste, coconut milk-cornflour mixture, sugar and salt.
3. Bring to a boil, add the prepared potlis and simmer for about 7 to 10 minutes.
4. Add the lemon juice and mix well. Remove from the fire.
   Serve hot.

~ **Dal Fry** ~

*C*reamy, rich and smooth. This is the perfect accompaniment for rice or rotis.

Preparation time : 10 minutes.   Cooking time : 25 minutes.   Serves 4.

1 cup masoor dal (split red lentils)
¼ cup yellow moong dal (split yellow lentils)
2 green chillies, slit
1 tsp grated ginger
1 tsp grated garlic
¼ tsp turmeric powder (haldi)
salt to taste

For the tempering
½ tsp mustard seeds (rai)
½ tsp nigella seeds (kalonji)
1 red chilli
1 onion, sliced
1 tomato, chopped

2 tbsp ghee

For the garnish
3 tbsp chopped coriander
1 tbsp butter

1. Wash the dals together.
2. Combine the dals, chillies, ginger, garlic, turmeric powder, salt and 3 cups of water and pressure cook till the dals are tender.
3. Remove the chillies and discard. Whisk the dal till it is smooth. Keep aside.

For the tempering
1. Heat the ghee in a pan and add the mustard seeds, nigella seeds and red chilli.
2. When the mustard seeds crackle, add the onion and sauté till it is translucent.
3. Add the tomato and sauté for another 3 to 4 minutes.

How to proceed
Add the dals to the tempering, mix well and bring to a boil.
Serve hot garnished with the chopped coriander and butter.

~ One Dish Dal ~

Picture on cover.

Vegetables simmered with pulses. A simple dish that needs no accompaniment other than rotis or rice.

Preparation time : 20 minutes.   Cooking time : 40 minutes.   Serves 4.

For the dal
2 tbsp yellow moong dal (split yellow lentils)
¼ cup masoor dal (split red lentils)
1 green chilli
1 tsp grated ginger
1 tsp grated garlic
½ tsp turmeric powder (haldi)

Other ingredients
6 to 8 bhindi (okra), cut into 25 mm. (1") pieces
½ cup cluster beans (gavar), cut into 25 mm. (1") pieces
1 carrot, diced
1 sweet corn, cut into circles
2 potatoes, diced

2 brinjals, diced
½ tsp cumin seeds (jeera)
6 to 8 curry leaves
½ tsp fenugreek (methi) seeds
¼ tsp asafoetida (hing)
1 tsp chilli powder
2 tbsp oil
salt to taste

For the dal
1. Wash the moong dal and masoor dal. Drain.
2. Pressure cook the dals, green chilli, ginger, garlic, turmeric powder, salt with 1 cup of water, till the dals are tender.

How to proceed
1. Whisk the pressure cooked dal till smooth and remove the green chilli.
2. Heat the oil in a large pan and add the cumin seeds, curry leaves, fenugreek seeds and asafoetida and stir for a few seconds.
3. Add the bhindi, cluster beans, carrots, sweet corn, potatoes, brinjal and chilli powder and sauté for 5 to 7 minutes till the vegetables soften.
4. Add the cooked dal and 1 cup of water and salt and simmer for 5 to 10 minutes. Serve hot.

Rice

~ .Tendli Bhaat ~

This Maharashtian recipe of rice and tendli simmered with spices makes a great meal by itself.

Preparation time : 10 minutes.   Cooking time : 20 minutes.   Serves 4.

1½ cups tendli, sliced horizontally
1 cup long grained rice
½ tsp mustard seeds (rai)
½ tsp cumin seeds (jeera)
3 cardamoms (elaichi)
12 mm.(½″) piece cinnamon (dalchini)
5 cloves (laung)
¼ tsp fenugreek (methi) seeds
2 green chillies, slit
5 curry leaves
¼ tsp asafoetida (hing)
½ tsp turmeric powder (haldi)

½ tsp chilli powder
¼ cup grated coconut
1 tbsp ghee
salt to taste

To be ground into a spice powder
3 cloves, roasted
25 mm. (1") piece cinnamon (dalchini)
2 tsp coriander seeds, roasted
2 tsp cumin seeds (jeera), roasted
1 tsp caraway seeds (shah jeera)
½ cup grated dry coconut (kopra)
¼ cup sesame seeds (til)

For the garnish
¼ cup grated coconut
2 tbsp chopped coriander
2 tbsp cashewnuts, fried

1. Wash and soak the rice for about 10 minutes. Drain and keep aside.
2. Heat the ghee and add the mustard seeds. When they crackle, add the cumin seeds,

cardamoms, cinnamon, cloves, fenugreek seeds, green chillies, curry leaves and asafoetida.

3. Add the tendli and rice and sauté for a few minutes.
4. Add the turmeric powder, chilli powder, half the spice powder and salt and mix well. Sauté for a further 2 minutes.
5. Add 2 cups of hot water and cook on slow flame till the rice is tender.
6. Add ¼ cup grated coconut and the remaining half of the spice powder. Cover and cook for about 2 minutes on a very slow flame.
   Serve hot garnished with the grated coconut, chopped coriander and the fried cashewnuts.

VARIATION : You can also use brinjals instead of tendli in this recipe to make VANGI BHAAT (picture on page 1) and peas to make VATANA BHAAT.

~ **Hariyali Chawal** ~

Coriander lends a delicate flavour to this rice. You can also use dill leaves along with coriander.

Preparation time : 10 minutes.   Cooking time : 10 minutes.   Serves 4.

1½ cups long grained rice
1½ cups chopped coriander
4 peppercorns
25 mm. (1") piece cinnamon (dalchini)
4 cloves (laung)
4 green cardamoms (elaichi)
2 onions, sliced
2 tbsp oil
salt to taste

For the garnish
¼ cup onion slices, browned

1. Wash and soak the rice for about 10 minutes. Drain and keep aside.
2. Heat the oil in a pressure cooker and add the peppercorns, cinnamon, cloves, green cardamoms and onions and sauté till the onions turn translucent.
3. Add the rice and sauté for a few minutes.
4. Add 3 cups of hot water and salt and pressure cook till the rice is tender.
5. Remove from the fire and add the chopped coriander. Mix well using a fork so that the rice grains do not break.
6. Garnish with the browned onion slices and serve hot.

Handy Tips : 1. The coriander is added last so that it retains its colour.
2. Crushed peanuts can be added for a better taste.

~ **Kofta Biryani** ~

*F*ragrant long-grained rice interlaced with a spinach gravy and chick peas koftas.

Preparation time : 20 minutes.   Cooking time : 1 hour.   Serves 4 to 6.

For the koftas
¾ cup soaked chick peas (Kabuli chana)
1 onion
1 green chilli
2 tbsp chopped coriander
3 cloves garlic
juice of ½ lemon
salt to taste
oil for cooking

For the gravy
1 onion, finely chopped
2 tomatoes, puréed
1 tsp grated ginger

½ tsp turmeric powder (haldi)
1 tsp chilli powder
¾ tsp garam masala
2 cups chopped spinach (palak)
⅓ cup cream
2 tbsp oil
salt to taste

For the rice
1 cup long-grained rice
2 cloves (laung)
2 bay leaves (tejpatta)
salt to taste

Other ingredients
½ cup chopped mint leaves
⅓ cup milk
1 tbsp butter
¼ tsp cardamom (elaichi) powder
a few strands of saffron

For the koftas
1. Combine all the ingredients except the oil in a blender and grind to a smooth paste.
2. Shallow fry spoonfuls of the mixture using oil on a non-stick pan over a medium flame, on both sides, till golden brown. Drain and keep aside.

For the gravy
1. Heat the oil a pan and sauté the onions till they turn translucent.
2. Add the tomato purée, ginger, turmeric powder and chilli powder and cook till the oil separates.
3. Add the garam masala and spinach and sauté for a further 2 minutes.
4. Add the cream and salt and mix well. Keep aside.

For the rice
1. Clean and wash the rice.
2. In a large pan, add the rice, cloves, bay leaves, salt and 2 cups of water.
3. Bring to a boil and simmer till the rice is almost cooked. Keep aside.

How to proceed

1. In a greased bowl, spread the half the rice to form one even layer.
2. Arrange all the koftas over the rice.
3. Spoon the gravy on top and sprinkle the mint leaves.
4. Spread another layer of rice.
5. In another pan, combine the milk, butter, cardamom powder and saffron and bring to a boil.
6. Pour over the layered biryani.
7. Cover with a tight lid and bake on a pre-heated oven at 200°C (400°F) for 20 minutes.

   Serve hot.

Handy Tip : The chick peas have to be soaked for at least 6 hours. ¼ cup raw chick peas will yield approx. ¾ cup of soaked chick peas.

~ Matki Pulao ~

Picture on facing page.

Moath and rice that are used in everyday cooking, surprisingly make a delectable dish.

Preparation time : 20 minutes.   Cooking time : 30 minutes.   Serves 4.

1 cup cooked long-grained rice
1 cup sprouted moath beans (matki), parboiled
2 cloves (laung)
¼ tsp asafoetida (hing)
1 green chilli, chopped
1 tsp grated ginger
½ capsicum, chopped
4 to 6 spring onions, chopped
¼ tsp turmeric powder (haldi)
1 tsp chilli powder
1 tsp coriander (dhania) powder
1 tbsp oil
salt to taste

MATKI PULAO : Recipe above ➙

For the garnish
1 tomato, chopped
2 tbsp chopped coriander

1. Heat the oil, add the cloves and asafoetida and sauté for a few seconds.
2. Add the green chilli, ginger, capsicum and spring onions and sauté for 2 to 3 minutes.
3. Add the turmeric powder, chilli powder, coriander powder and moath beans and mix well.
4. Add ¼ cup of water and the salt and simmer over a slow flame till the moath beans are cooked.
5. Add the rice and toss well.
   Serve hot garnished with the chopped tomato and coriander.

Handy Tip : To sprout moath beans - soak in water for 6-8 hrs. and then tie them in a damp muslin cloth. They will sprout in about 24-36 hrs. in warm weather.

~ Nariyalwale Chawal ~

Rice and creamy coconut milk make a unique combination.

Preparation time : 10 minutes.   Cooking time : 20 minutes.   Serves 4.

1¼ cups long grained rice
1 tbsp urad dal (split black gram)
2 tbsp yellow moong dal (split yellow gram)
6 red chillies
4 to 5 curry leaves
2 tbsp salted peanuts, crushed lightly
2½ cups (500 ml.) coconut milk
2 tbsp oil
salt to taste

For the garnish
¼ cup grated coconut

1. Clean, wash and soak the rice for about 20 minutes. Drain and keep aside.

2. Heat the oil in a pressure cooker. Add the urad dal and moong dal and fry for 2 minutes.
3. Add the red chillies, curry leaves and peanuts and fry again for about 1 minute.
4. Add the rice and sauté for a further 2 to 3 minutes.
5. Add the coconut milk and salt and pressure cook for 2 whistles.
   Serve hot garnished with the grated coconut.

Handy Tip : You can also garnish this dish with chopped onions and tomatoes.

~ **Badshahi Khichdi** ~

A khichdi layered with a potato vegetable topped with tempered curds makes a meal by itself.

Preparation time : 10 minutes.   Cooking time : 30 minutes.   Serves 4.

For the rice
1 cup rice
½ cup toovar (arhar) dal
2 cloves (laung)
1 stick cinnamon (dalchini)
a pinch asafoetida (hing)
¼ tsp turmeric powder (haldi)
2 tbsp ghee
salt to taste

For the potato vegetable
4 medium sized potatoes, boiled, peeled and diced
1 tsp ginger-green chilli paste
1 tsp mustard seeds (rai)

2 onions, sliced
¼ tsp turmeric powder (haldi)
1 tsp chilli powder
1 tsp coriander (dhania) powder
3 tbsp fresh curds
2 tbsp ghee
salt to taste

For the tempered curds
1 cup fresh curds
1 tsp mustard seeds (rai)
4 to 6 curry leaves
1 tsp ghee
salt to taste

For the garnish
2 tbsp chopped coriander

For the rice
1. Clean, wash and soak the rice and toovar dal for about 30 minutes. Drain and keep aside.
2. Heat the ghee in a pressure cooker, add the cloves and cinnamon and stir-fry for

42

half a minute. Then add the asafoetida and turmeric powder.
3. Add the rice, toovar dal, salt and 4 cups of hot water and pressure cook till the rice is slightly over-cooked. Keep aside.

For the potato vegetable
1. Heat the ghee in a pan and add the mustard seeds to it. When they crackle, add the onions and fry for some time till they turn translucent.
2. Add the ginger-green chilli paste, turmeric powder, chilli powder, coriander powder and sauté for 1 to 2 minutes.
3. Add the potatoes and salt and sauté for some more time.
4. Add the curds, mix well and keep aside.

For the tempered curds
1. Whisk the curds with the salt and keep aside.
2. Heat the ghee in a small pan and add the mustard seeds to it.
3. When they crackle, add the curry leaves and pour over the curds. Mix well.

How to proceed
1. Place the potato vegetable at the bottom of a serving dish.
2. Top with a layer of the rice over it.
3. Pour the curds on top and garnish with the chopped coriander.
   Serve hot.

Subzis

~ **Cauliflower and Potato Ghasi** ~

Picture on page 19.

This authentic Manglorean recipe tastes great with steamed rice.

Preparation time : 15 minutes.   Cooking time : 30 minutes.   Serves 4.

2 cups cauliflower florets
1 cup potatoes, peeled and cut into cubes
1 tsp ginger paste
¼ cup chopped onions
½ cup (100 ml.) coconut milk
1 tbsp oil
salt to taste

To be ground into a paste
¾ cup grated coconut
¼ cup chopped onions
3 red chillies, broken into pieces
2 tsp coriander (dhania) seeds
¼ tsp mustard seeds (rai)

45

a pinch fenugreek (methi) seeds
¼ tsp cumin seeds (jeera)
25 mm. (1") piece cinnamon (dalchini)
4 peppercorns
2 cloves (laung)
½ tsp turmeric powder (haldi)
½ tsp tamarind (imli) pulp
2 tbsp oil

For the paste
1. Heat the oil in a pan and sauté the onions and coconut till the onions turn translucent.
2. Dry roast the red chillies, coriander seeds, mustard seeds, fenugreek seeds, cumin seeds, cinnamon, peppercorns and cloves in a pan and keep aside.
3. Grind the coconut, onions, dry spices, turmeric powder and tamarind pulp to a smooth paste. Keep aside.

How to proceed
1. Heat the oil in a kadhai, add the ginger paste and onions and sauté till the onions turn translucent.
2. Add the cauliflower, potatoes, salt and ¾ cup of water and cook on a medium

flame till the vegetables are tender.
3. Add the paste and coconut milk and simmer for some more time.
   Serve hot.

Handy Tip : Diced brinjal can be used instead of cauliflower as a variation.

～ **Soya Mutter ki Subzi** ～

*S*oyabean nuggets and peas simmered in a tangy gravy.

Preparation time : 10 minutes.   Cooking time : 40 minutes.   Serves 2.

½ cup soya nuggets
½ cup green peas
½ tsp cumin seeds (jeera)
a pinch asafoetida (hing)
1 tsp ginger-green chilli paste
½ tsp garlic paste
2 medium onions, chopped
2 tomatoes, finely chopped
¼ tsp turmeric powder (haldi)
½ tsp chilli powder
½ tsp coriander (dhania) powder
¼ cup fresh curds
2 tsp Bengal gram flour (besan)
2 tbsp milk

½ tsp sugar
2 tbsp oil
salt to taste

1. Cook the soya nuggets in hot salted water for about 20 minutes. Keep aside.
2. Heat the oil and add the cumin seeds. When they crackle, add the asafoetida, ginger-green chilli paste, garlic paste and onions and sauté till the onions turn translucent.
3. Add the tomatoes, turmeric powder, chilli powder and coriander powder and cook on a slow flame for about 5 to 10 minutes.
4. Mix the curds, gram flour, milk and ¾ cup of water and add to the onion-tomato gravy.
5. Add the soya nuggets, green peas, sugar and salt and simmer for 2 more minutes. Serve hot.

VARIATION : You can use mushrooms or paneer instead of the soya nuggets.

~ **Tilwale Alu** ~

S*esame seeds and potatoes make a great combination.*

Preparation time : 10 minutes.   Cooking time : 15 minutes.   Serves 4.

16 baby potatoes
1/8 tsp cumin seeds (jeera)
1/2 tsp mustards seeds (rai)
4 to 6 curry leaves
2 tsp ginger-green chilli paste
1/4 tsp turmeric powder (haldi)
2 tbsp sesame seeds (til), roasted
1 tsp lemon juice
2 tbsp oil
salt to taste

For the garnish
1 tbsp chopped coriander
1 green chilli, chopped

1. Parboil the potatoes in salted water. Peel and keep aside.
2. Heat the oil in a non-stick pan and add the cumin seeds, mustard seeds and curry leaves. When the seeds crackle, add the ginger-green chilli paste and stir for some time.
3. Add the potatoes, turmeric powder and salt and sauté for 4 to 5 minutes.
4. Add ½ cup of water and cook on a slow flame till all the moisture has evaporated and the potatoes are cooked.
5. Remove from the fire, add the sesame seeds and lemon juice and mix well.
6. Garnish with the chopped coriander and green chilli and serve hot.

～ **Baby Corn Paneer Jalfrazie** ～

Baby corn and paneer tossed in tomato capsicum gravy.

Preparation time : 10 minutes.   Cooking time : 15 minutes.   Serves 4.

12 nos. baby corn, cut into 4 lengthwise
1¼ cups paneer, cut into 25 mm. (1") strips
¼ tsp cumin seeds (jeera)
⅛ tsp asafoetida (hing)
1 tsp ginger-green chilli paste
3 spring onions whites, sliced
3 spring onion greens, chopped
½ green capsicum, sliced
½ red capsicum, sliced
¼ tsp turmeric powder (haldi)
½ tsp chilli powder
1 large tomato, puréed
1 tbsp tomato purée (optional)
2 tbsp chopped coriander

1 tbsp oil
salt to taste

1. Heat the oil in a pan and add the cumin seeds and asafoetida. When they crackle, add the ginger-green chilli paste, spring onion whites and capsicums and sauté for 2 minutes.
2. Add the baby corn, turmeric powder, chilli powder, tomato, tomato purée and salt and sauté on a slow flame for 4 to 5 minutes till the baby corn is cooked.
3. Add the paneer and spring onion greens and toss lightly.
   Garnish with the chopped coriander and serve hot.

~ **Jhat-Pat Subzi** ~

Picture on facing page.

Vegetables and chick peas tossed in sesame seeds and chilli sauce. Simple, yet delicious.

Preparation time : 20 minutes.   Cooking time : 10 minutes.   Serves 4.

6 baby potatoes, peeled and boiled
8 baby onions, peeled
6 nos. baby corn
1 carrot, peeled
1 cucumber, peeled
6 cherry tomatoes
½ cup cooked chick peas (Kabuli chana)
1½ tbsp sesame seeds (til)
1 tsp ginger paste
1 tsp garlic paste
1 tbsp chilli sauce
1 tsp chilli flakes (paprika)
1 tbsp oil

JHAT-PAT SUBZI : Recipe above →

salt to taste

1. Cut the baby corn, carrot and cucumber into thick strips like French fries. Keep aside.
2. Heat the oil in a pan and add the sesame seeds to it.
3. When they crackle, add the ginger paste and garlic paste and sauté for some time.
4. Add all the vegetables, chick peas and salt and stir.
5. Add the chilli sauce and chilli flakes and mix well.
   Serve hot.

～ **Subzi Pasanda** ～

Sautéed paneer and capsicum in a truly unusual gravy of puréed sweet corn.

Preparation time : 10 minutes.   Cooking time : 20 minutes.   Serves 4.

3 capsicums, thinly sliced
1½ cups cubed paneer (cottage cheese)
1 cup sweet corn kernels
1 tsp cumin seeds (jeera)
¼ tsp asafoetida (hing)
1 tsp chopped green chillies
1½ tsp grated ginger
a pinch sugar
3 tbsp chopped coriander
3 tbsp oil
salt to taste

1. Purée the sweet corn kernels with ½ cup of water into a fine paste in a blender and keep aside.
2. Heat 2 tbsp of oil in a pan and sauté the capsicums and paneer till they are lightly browned. Remove and keep aside.
3. Heat the remaining 1 tbsp of oil in the same pan and add the cumin seeds and asafoetida.
4. When the cumin seeds crackle, add the green chillies and ginger, sauté for a few seconds and add the puréed corn.
5. Add 1½ cups of water, sugar and salt and bring it to a boil.
6. Add the sautéed capsicum, paneer and coriander and mix well.
   Serve hot with parathas.

Farsans

~ **Masala Bhindi** ~

S*picy, deep-fried ladies fingers. A spicy accompaniment to dal and chawal.*

Preparation time : 10 minutes.   Cooking time : 10 minutes.   Serves 4.

2 cups bhindi (ladies fingers), slit into four lengthwise
2 tbsp Bengal gram flour (besan)
½ tsp turmeric powder (haldi)
1 tsp chilli powder
2 tsp chaat masala
1 tsp lemon juice
salt to taste

Other ingredients
oil for deep frying

1. Mix together all the ingredients in a bowl. Toss well.
2. Heat the oil in a kadhai and deep fry the bhindi till crisp.
3. Drain on absorbent paper.

Serve hot.

Handy Tips : 1. These have to be fried almost immediately after you mix them as otherwise they will not be crisp as the bhindi will release water, making them soggy.
2. For the garnish, you may use chopped red capsicum and coriander to enhance its eye appeal.

~ Makai ka Dhokla ~

Scrumptious sweet corn and maize flour dhoklas ready within minutes.

Preparation time : 30 minutes.   Cooking time : 25 minutes.   Serves 4.

1 cup maize flour (makai ka atta)
½ cup sour curds
½ cup sweet corn kernels
2 tsp ginger-green chilli paste
¼ tsp asafoetida (hing)
2 tsp sugar
1 tsp lemon juice
1 tsp fruit salt
2 tsp oil
salt to taste

For the tempering
1 tsp mustard seeds (rai)
1 tsp sesame seeds (til)

a pinch asafoetida (hing)
1 tbsp oil

Other ingredients
oil for greasing

For the garnish
1 tbsp chopped coriander

1. Combine the maize flour and sour curds with ½ cup of warm water in a bowl. Mix well to make a smooth batter. Keep aside for at least 30 minutes.
2. Add the sweet corn, ginger-green chilli paste, asafoetida, sugar, lemon juice, oil and salt and mix well.
3. Add the fruit salt, mix gently and pour the batter into a greased 150 mm. (6") diameter thali. Steam for 15 to 20 minutes.
4. Prepare the tempering by heating the oil, adding the mustard seeds, sesame seeds and asafoetida and frying until the seeds crackle. Pour the tempering over the prepared dhokla.
5. Garnish with the chopped coriander. Cut into pieces and serve hot.

Handy Tip : Add the fruit salt just before you put the dhoklas to steam.

~ Chat-Pata Pav ~

Picture on facing page.

A spicy way to serve bread. Quick and easy.

Preparation time : 5 minutes.   Cooking time : 20 minutes.   Makes 4.

4 ladi pavs, cut into half
2 tbsp butter

For the masala
1 large onion, chopped
½ capsicum, chopped
2 cloves garlic
2 tomatoes, chopped
½ tsp turmeric powder (haldi)
½ tsp chilli powder
½ tsp black salt (sanchal)
½ tsp garam masala
2 tbsp butter
salt to taste

CHAT-PATA PAV : Recipe above →

For the garnish
2 tbsp chopped coriander
lemon wedges

For the masala
1. Heat the butter in a pan and sauté the onions and capsicum, till they are translucent.
2. Add the garlic, tomatoes, turmeric powder and chilli powder and sauté for a further 5 minutes.
3. Add the black salt and garam masala and mix well. Keep aside.

How to proceed
1. Heat the butter on a tava (griddle) and grill the pav on both sides till crisp.
2. Add the cooked masala and coat the pav in it.
   Serve hot garnished with the chopped coriander and lemon wedges.

~ **Dhokla Simla Mirch** ~

*C*apsicum *halves filled with khaman dhokla.*

Preparation time : 10 minutes.   Cooking time : 15 minutes.   Serves 4 to 6.

8 large capsicums
1 packet instant khaman dhokla

For the tempering
1 tsp mustard seeds (rai)
1 tsp sesame seeds (til)
a pinch asafoetida (hing)
4 to 6 curry leaves
2 tbsp oil

For the garnish
2 tbsp chopped coriander

1. Cut the capsicums into 2 halves vertically. Remove the seeds carefully so as to retain the shape of the halves.
2. Make the khaman dhokla as per the directions on the packet.
3. Pour the khaman dhokla mixture into each capsicum half. Steam for 10 minutes.
4. Allow the capsicums to cool. Cut each capsicum half into 2 pieces.
5. Heat the oil in a pan, add the mustard seeds and when they crackle, add the sesame seeds, asafoetida and curry leaves.
6. Add the capsicum pieces and sauté for 4 to 5 minutes.
   Serve hot garnished with the chopped coriander.

Rotis

~ Jowar Pyaz ki Roti ~

Jowar rotis flavoured with onions and green chilli.

Preparation time : 5 minutes.　Cooking time : 20 minutes.　Makes 4 rotis.

1 cup jowar flour (white millet flour)
1 spring onion, finely chopped
1 green chilli, finely chopped
1 tbsp oil
salt to taste

1. Combine all the ingredients in a bowl and knead into a soft dough using warm
   water if required.
2. Cover and keep aside for 10 minutes.
3. Divide the dough into 4 equal portions.
4. Pat each portion on a dry surface using your palm till it is a circle of 125 mm. (5")
   diameter.
5. Cook on a tava (griddle) till both sides are lightly browned.

Serve hot with a vegetable of your choice.

Handy Tip : If you want to roll out these rotis, you can do so between 2 sheets of plastic.

~ Kaddu Palak ki Roti ~

Spinach and red pumpkin make delicious chapatis.

Preparation time : 10 minutes.   Cooking time : 15 minutes.   Makes 5 rotis.

1 cup peeled and grated red pumpkin (kaddu)
1 cup chopped spinach (palak)
1 cup whole wheat flour (gehun ka atta)
1 tsp chilli powder
½ green chilli, chopped
¼ tsp turmeric powder (haldi)
1 tbsp oil
salt to taste

Other ingredients
oil for cooking

1. Heat the oil, add the spinach and sauté for 2 minutes.
2. Remove from the fire.

72

3. Mix all the other ingredients to make a soft dough using enough water. Knead well.
4. Divide the dough into 5 equal portions.
5. Roll out each portion into a circle of 125 mm. (5") diameter.
6. Heat a tava (griddle) and cook each roti on both sides, until golden brown using a little oil.
   Serve hot.

~ Dal Paratha ~

Picture on facing page.

Wheat flour parathas stuffed with a spicy moong dal filling.

Preparation time : 10 minutes.   Cooking time : 30 minutes.   Makes 6 parathas.

For the dough
1 cup whole wheat flour (gehun ka atta)
1 tsp oil
salt to taste

For the filling
½ cup yellow moong dal (split yellow gram)
½ tsp cumin seeds (jeera)
¼ tsp asafoetida (hing)
¼ tsp turmeric powder (haldi)
¾ tsp chilli powder
1 tsp oil
salt to taste

DAL PARATHA : Recipe above →

Other ingredients
oil for cooking

For the dough
1. Combine all the ingredients and knead into a soft dough using enough water.
2. Divide into 6 equal portions and keep aside.

For the filling
1. Wash and soak the dal for at least 20 minutes. Drain.
2. Cook the dal in ¾ cup of water till all the water is absorbed.
3. Heat the oil in a pan and add the cumin seeds. When they crackle, add the asafoetida, cooked dal, turmeric powder, chilli powder and salt.
4. Simmer till the dal mixture is dry, stirring continuously.
5. Cool completely and divide into 6 equal portions.

How to proceed
1. Roll out one portion of the dough into a 100 mm. (4") diameter circle.
2. Place one portion of the filling mixture in the centre of the circle.
3. Bring together all the sides in the centre and seal tightly.
4. Roll out again into a circle of 150 mm. (6") diameter, using flour to roll the paratha.
5. Cook on a tava (griddle), using a little oil, until both sides are golden brown.
6. Repeat with the remaining dough and filling to make 5 more parathas. Serve hot.

~ **Phudina Puris** ~

*M*int and cumin seeds impart a distinctive flavour to these tasty puris.

Preparation time : 10 minutes.   Cooking time : 20 minutes.   Makes 15 puris.

2 cups plain flour (maida)
½ cup mint leaves (phudina)
1 tsp cumin seeds (jeera)
2 green chillies, chopped
1 tbsp lemon juice
1 tsp sugar
salt to taste
oil for greasing and deep frying

1. Pound the mint leaves, cumin seeds, green chillies, lemon juice, sugar and salt together in a mortar and pestle.
2. Combine this mixture with the flour, add enough water and knead into a firm

dough. Divide into 15 equal portions.
3. Roll out on a lightly greased surface into thin circles of 75 mm. (3") diameter.
4. Deep fry in hot oil till golden brown and drain on absorbent paper.
   Serve hot.

Handy Tip : You can also make parathas with the same dough.

~ **Paneer Masoor Paratha** ~

Paratha envelopes filled with lentils and cottage cheese.

Preparation time : 15 minutes.   Cooking time : 45 minutes.   Makes 4 parathas.

For the dough
½ cup whole wheat flour (gehun ka atta)
1 tbsp oil
salt to taste

For the filling
½ cup crumbled paneer (cottage cheese)
2 tbsp whole masoor (whole red lentils), cooked
1 onion, chopped
1 tsp grated ginger
½ tsp chilli powder
½ tsp turmeric powder (haldi)
1 tsp coriander (dhania) powder
2 tbsp chopped coriander

1 tbsp oil
salt to taste

Other ingredients
oil for cooking

For the dough
1. Combine all the ingredients and knead into a soft dough using enough water.
2. Cover with a wet cloth and keep aside for 10 to 15 minutes.

For the filling
1. Heat the oil and sauté the onions till they turn translucent.
2. Add the paneer, masoor, ginger, chilli powder, turmeric powder, coriander powder, coriander and salt and mix well.
3. Cool, divide into 4 parts. Keep aside.

How to proceed
1. Divide the dough into 4 equal parts and roll out each portion very thinly into circles of 250 mm. (10") diameter.
2. Put one portion of the stuffing in the centre of each paratha and fold all the sides in such a way so as to form a rectangle.

3. Make a paste using a little flour and water and use this to seal the edges of the paratha.
4. Place the paratha on a tava (griddle) with the open edge at the bottom. Cook for a few minutes, turn over on the other side and cook again till crispy, using a little oil.
5. Repeat for the remaining dough and filling to make 3 more parathas.
   Serve hot with curds.

~ **Makai ki Roti** ~

Picture on page 2.

A bread made of fresh sweet corn and spices.

Preparation time : 10 minutes.   Cooking time : 15 minutes.   Makes 6 rotis.

½ cup sweet corn kernels
½ cup whole wheat flour (gehun ka atta)
¼ tsp chilli powder
¼ tsp cumin seeds (jeera)
½ tsp lemon juice
¼ cup chopped coriander
½ tsp sugar
1 tbsp oil
salt to taste

Other ingredients
oil for cooking
butter to serve

82

1. Grind half the sweet corn kernels to a fine paste in a food processor (without using any water).
2. Mix the sweet corn paste with the rest of the ingredients in a bowl using water only if needed and make a soft dough.
3. Divide the dough into 6 equal portions.
4. Roll out each portion into a circle of 100 mm. (4") diameter.
5. Heat a tava (griddle) and cook each roti on both sides on a slow flame until golden brown using a little oil.

   Serve hot topped with a dollop of butter.

Mithais

SEV BIRANJ : Recipe on page 86 →

84

~ **Sev Biranj** ~

Picture on page 85.

Vermicelli cooked in milk and sugar and flavoured with cardamom and saffron.

Preparation time : 5 minutes.   Cooking time : 15 minutes.   Serves 4.

1 cup crushed vermicelli (sevian)
¼ cup milk
½ cup sugar
2 to 3 strands saffron
¼ tsp cardamom (elaichi) powder
3 tbsp ghee

For the garnish
2 tbsp slivered pistachios

1. Heat the ghee in a heavy bottomed pan, add the vermicelli and cook on a slow
   flame for 5 to 7 minutes until the vermicelli is golden brown in colour.
2. Add the milk and 1 cup of water and cook for a further 5 minutes.

3. Add the sugar, saffron, cardamom powder and cook till the sugar has completely dissolved.
4. Garnish with slivered pistachios.
   Serve hot.

~ **Kalakand** ~

An instant version of the traditional dessert.

Preparation time : 10 minutes.   Cooking time : 15 minutes.
Makes about 16 pieces.

¾ cup paneer (cottage cheese), unsalted
8 tbsp whole milk powder
¼ cup sugar
½ cup cream
½ tsp cardamom (elaichi) powder

For the garnish
10 almonds, slivered

1. Combine all the ingredients in a non-stick pan.
2. Cook over a medium flame, stirring continuously for approx. 10 to 15 minutes till
   the mixture thickens.

3. Spread onto a 175 mm. (7") diameter pie dish. Cool and cut into 16 pieces.
4. Garnish with slivered almonds and serve chilled.

Handy Tip : Use fresh paneer for best results.

~ **Mock Almond Halwa** ~

A scrumptious dessert made from Bengal gram and almonds.

Preparation time : 5 minutes.   Cooking time : 30 minutes.   Serves 4.

¾ cup split Bengal gram (chana dal)
½ cup milk
½ cup sugar
2 to 3 strands saffron
1 drop almond essence
4 tbsp ghee

For the garnish
4 tbsp chopped almonds (roasted)

1. Clean, wash and soak the Bengal gram for at least 2 hours.
2. Drain the Bengal gram and grind it in a food processor to a coarse paste.
3. Heat the ghee in a heavy bottomed pan and add the Bengal gram paste. Cook on a slow flame, while stirring continuously till it turns golden brown in colour.

4. Add the milk, sugar, saffron and 1 cup of water, continue cooking on slow flame till the sugar has dissolved (about 10 minutes), stirring continuously.
5. Remove from the fire, add the almond essence and mix well.
6. Garnish with the chopped almonds and serve hot.

~ Instant Jalebis ~

A quick variation of the traditional dessert.

Preparation time : 10 minutes.   Cooking time : 15 minutes.   Makes 15 jalebis.

For the jalebi batter
1 cup plain flour (maida)
1 tsp Bengal gram flour (besan)
½ tsp crumbled fresh yeast
1 tbsp melted ghee
1 tsp sugar
2 to 3 drops of lemon yellow food colouring

For the sugar syrup
½ cup sugar
a few strands saffron
¼ tsp lemon juice

Other ingredients
ghee for deep frying

For the jalebi batter
1. Sieve the flour and gram flour together.
2. Dissolve the yeast in 1 tbsp of water.
3. Mix the flour mixture, yeast solution, ghee, sugar and lemon yellow food colouring with ⅔ cup of water to make a thick batter, making sure no lumps remain.
4. Keep aside for 10 minutes.

For the sugar syrup
1. Dissolve the sugar with ½ cup of water and simmer for 5 minutes till the syrup is of 2 string consistency.
2. Add the saffron and lemon juice and mix.
3. Remove from the fire and keep aside.

How to proceed
1. Heat the ghee in a broad saucepan [the ghee should be approximately 25 mm. (1") deep].
2. Fill the jalebi batter into a piping bag with a single hole nozzle or a thick cloth with a small hole in the centre which is finished with button-hole stitch.

3. Press out round whirls into the hot ghee working closely from outside to the centre of the whirl (approx. 50 mm [2″] diameter).
4. Deep fry the jalebis till golden brown and transfer into warm sugar syrup.
5. Drain immediately and serve hot.

Handy Tip : Do not allow the jalebi batter to overferment. Fry the jalebis immediately once the batter has rested for 10 minutes.

~ Makhane ki Kheer ~

*L*otus seeds simmered in milk and flavoured with nutmeg.

Preparation time : 10 minutes.   Cooking time : 25 minutes.   Serves 4.

1 cup makhanas (lotus seeds)
5 cups milk
2 tbsp ghee
¾ cup sugar
½ tsp nutmeg (jaiphal) powder
3 to 4 strands saffron

For the garnish
1 tbsp slivered pistachios
2 to 3 glace cherries, sliced
1 edible silver leaf (varq)

1. Heat the ghee in a pan, add the makhanas and sauté for 3 to 4 minutes till they are crisp.

95

2. Remove from the fire and crush them slightly.
3. Heat the milk in a heavy bottomed pan and when it comes to a boil, add the crushed makhanas and simmer for about 15 to 20 minutes.
4. Add the nutmeg powder and saffron. Mix well.
5. Remove from the fire.
6. Garnish with the slivered pistachios, glace cherries and edible silver leaf. Serve hot.

Accompaniments

~ Kaddu ka Raita ~

*Y*ou have to taste this dish to believe how wonderful it is ! It tastes great with a spicy paratha.

Preparation time : 10 minutes.   Cooking time : 15 minutes.   Serves 4.

2 cups finely chopped red pumpkin (kaddu)
1 tsp cumin seeds (jeera)
2 to 3 green chillies, chopped
1 tsp sugar
1 cup fresh curds
1 tbsp ghee
salt to taste

For the garnish
2 tsp chopped coriander
1 tbsp roasted peanuts, crushed

1. Heat the ghee and add the cumin seeds.

2. When they crackle, add the green chillies and sauté for 15 seconds.
3. Add the pumpkin and sauté for 10 to 12 minutes till it is cooked.
4. Add the sugar and salt and mix well.
5. Mash lightly and cool completely.
6. Whisk the curds till smooth and add to the cooked pumpkin. Mix well.
   Serve chilled garnished with the chopped coriander and crushed peanuts.

~ **Mint Raita** ~

A simple accompaniment for your favourite paratha.

Preparation time : 5 minutes. No cooking. Serves 4.

¼ cup chopped mint (phudina) leaves
1 cup fresh curds
2 green chillies, chopped
1 tsp sugar
salt to taste

1. Blend all the ingredients in a food processor.
2. Chill and serve.

Handy Tip : You can add more sugar if you wish.

~ Til aur Khira ~

Diced cucumber lightly sautéed in black sesame seeds and crushed peanuts.

Preparation time : 5 minutes.   Cooking time : 5 minutes.   Serves 4.

2 medium cucumbers, peeled
½ tsp cumin seeds (jeera)
1 green chilli, slit
¼ tsp asafoetida (hing)
1½ tbsp black sesame seeds (kala til), roasted
1½ tbsp crushed and roasted peanuts
2 tbsp chopped coriander
1 tsp oil
salt to taste

1. Cut the cucumber into small cubes.
2. Heat the oil in a pan and add the cumin seeds, green chilli and asafoetida.
3. When the cumin seeds crackle, add the cucumber and salt and remove from the fire.

101

4. Add the sesame seeds, peanuts and coriander and toss well.
   Serve at room temperature.

Mini Series by *Tarla Dalal*

7 Dinner Menus

Forever Young Diet

Nutritious Recipes for Pregnancy

Healthy Subzis

High Blood Pressure Cookbook

Low Calorie Sweets

Good Food for Diabetes

Healthy Snacks for Kids

Iron Rich Recipes

Low Cholesterol Recipes

Healthy Juices

Healthy Breakfast

Healthy Snacks

Healthy Soups & Salads

Calcium Rich Recipes

Home Remedies

Fast Foods made Healthy